INSECTS

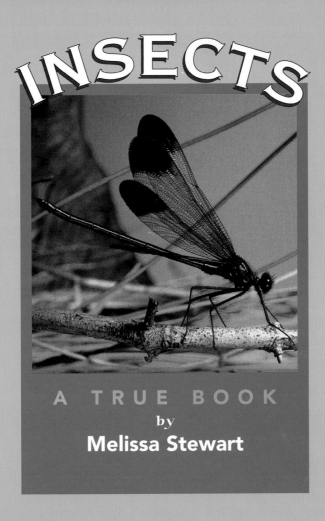

A TRUE BOOK

by
Melissa Stewart

Children's Press®
A Division of Grolier Publishing

New York London Hong Kong Sydney
Danbury, Connecticut

In the winter, monarch butterflies travel to warm parts of the world. Large numbers of these insects often perch together on trees.

Content Consultants
Jan Jenner, Ph.D.

Jeff Hahn, Ph.D.
Department of Entomology
University of Minnesota

The photograph on the cover shows a green darner dragonfly (right) and a katydid (left). The photograph on the title page shows a tipped-wing damsel fly.

Visit Children's Press® on
the Internet at:
http://publishing.grolier.com

Library of Congress Cataloging-in-Publication Data

Stewart, Melissa.
    Insects / by Melissa Stewart.
        p. cm. — (A true book)
    Includes bibliographical references and index.
    Summary: Describes the appearance, behavior, and life cycle of various insects, such as the green stink bug, the grasshopper, and the flea.
    ISBN: 0-516-22040-3 (lib. bdg.) 0-516-25951-2 (pbk.)
    Insects—Juvenile literature. [1. Insects.] I. Title. II. Series
QL467.2 .S777 2001
595.7—dc21
                                        99-087052
                                            CIP
                                            AC

GROLIER
PUBLISHING

Contents

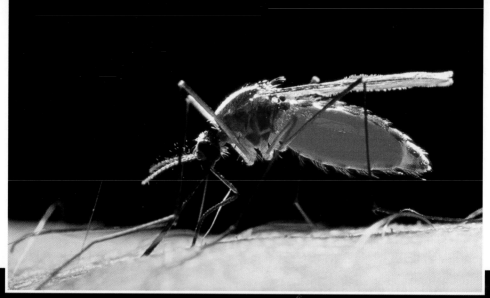

This mosquito (top) is sucking blood from a person, and this butterfly (bottom) is drinking nectar from a flower.

What Is an Insect?

What do you think of when you hear the word "insect?" Do you imagine a mosquito buzzing around your head? Maybe you picture a butterfly resting on a brightly colored flower.

There are more than one million different kinds of insects. Believe it or not, three out of

Some insects, such as this red-banded leafhopper, are colorful.

every four animals in the world are insects. For every person alive, there may be as many as 200 million insects.

Insects are small animals with three-part bodies, six legs, and a hard outer coat called an exoskeleton. An exoskeleton is like a suit of armor. It helps protect the insect from enemies. It also keeps an insect's insides moist. Other animals, such as lobsters and scorpions, have exoskeletons too.

If you accidentally step on this ground beetle, its exoskeleton will make a crunching noise.

What Is a

All bugs are insects, but not all insects are bugs. Confused? Think of it this way—a bug is a kind of insect, just like a butterfly or a beetle. Most bugs carry their wings crossed over their backs. They overlap to make an "X." The bodies of many bugs are shaped like a shield.

Bug?

Look at the pictures on these two pages. Which insect do you think is a bug? If you guessed the green stink bug (left), you were right. A ladybug (right) is really a kind of beetle.

An Insect's Head

An insect's body has three main parts—the head, the thorax (THOR-aks), and the abdomen (AB-duh-men). Each part is made up of segments— a series of small parts that fit together. The segments make it possible for an insect to bend its body.

Abdomen   Thorax   Head

Can you guess how this grasshopper's body parts help it bend?

Most insects have eyes, mouthparts, and antennae (an-TEN-ee) on their heads. Many insects have three simple eyes on the top of their head and two huge compound eyes. Scientists think the simple eyes on top of an insect's head can sense light and dark. The simple eyes cannot see objects.

Compound eyes are made up of many tiny lenses. A dragonfly may have as many

Look at how many tiny green lenses there are in this robber fly's compound eyes.

as 28,000 lenses in each eye. Each lens sees a small part of the object an insect is looking at. The insect's brain combines all the parts into a single image. Compound eyes are good for judging distances and noticing small movements.

Insects have different kinds of mouthparts. Zebra butter-flies use their mouthparts to suck up flower juices and tree sap. Box elder bugs can pierce the leaves of trees and suck

This tiger beetle is using its powerful jaws to eat another insect.

out the juices with their mouthparts. Tiger beetles have powerful jaws for chewing on smaller insects.

Most insects have a pair of antennae between their compound eyes. Antennae tell an insect about its surroundings. All insects use antennae to feel and smell. Some use them to taste and hear too.

Antennae come in many shapes and sizes. Cave crickets have long antennae to help them find their way in the dark. A butterfly's antennae have a bump on the end. Moths have feathery antennae.

A luna moth uses its feathery antennae to smell.

A June beetle's antennae have fingerlike parts attached to the ends.

The Thorax and Abdomen

An insect's legs and wings are attached to its thorax. When an insect walks or runs, it always has three legs on the ground—two on one side of its body and one on the other side. This helps the insect keep its balance.

The diving beetle's front legs help it to swim.

Insects have different kinds of legs. Giant water bugs, back swimmers, and diving beetles have long, flat back legs that work like oars. Grasshoppers, locusts, and fleas use their long, strong back legs for jumping. Fleas are great jumpers. If you could jump as well as a flea, you would be able to jump the length of two and one-half football fields. The strong, flat front legs of dung beetles are perfect for digging. Honeybees have little baskets on their back legs to carry sweet pollen from flowers. Crickets have ears on their legs, and butterflies taste with their feet.

These ants and aphids do not have wings.

Most insects have two pairs of wings. Flies have only one pair. Most ants and aphids have no wings at all. Wings help insects find food and escape from enemies. Some butterflies can fly more than 75 miles (121 kilometers) in a single day. The fastest insects are dragonflies. They can fly up to 60 miles (97 km) per hour.

The abdomen is the biggest part of an insect's body. It contains organs that are important for breaking down food and producing young insects. Many insects

Look at the earwig's feelers at the end of its abdomen. Some people think these feelers are poisonous, but that is not true.

have feelers at the end of their abdomens. A mayfly's feelers are very long. An earwig's feelers are sharp and can give a painful pinch.

That's Not

Ticks, spiders, and centipedes all look a little bit like insects, so you might be surprised to hear that they belong to different groups of animals. Remember, all insects have six legs and three-part bodies.

Ticks and spiders belong to a group called arachnids (ah-RAK-nidz). They have eight legs and their bodies have two main sections. Centipedes are in a group all by themselves. A centipede can have dozens of legs. It is hard to tell where a centipede's head ends and the rest of its body begins.

Count the legs of the spider (top) and centipede (bottom). Are they insects?

an Insect!

Where Insects Live

Insects are found all over the world. They live in some of the coldest, hottest, windiest, and wettest places you can think of. Small wingless moths live in Antarctica and can survive in very cold temperatures. In Africa, fog-drinking beetles live in the hot, dry Namib

The fog-drinking beetle lives in the Namib Desert, where temperatures can reach 150 degrees Fahrenheit (65.5 degrees Celsius) on the surface of the sand.

Desert. Young petroleum flies live in pools of crude oil in California.

Most insects live on or near plants, but some live in ponds and streams or underground. You can even find them inside your house. Can you guess where bed bugs live? Insects can live in so many places because they are small and have special body parts that help them find food, have young, and trick their enemies. Insects eat many different kinds of food, including plants, blood,

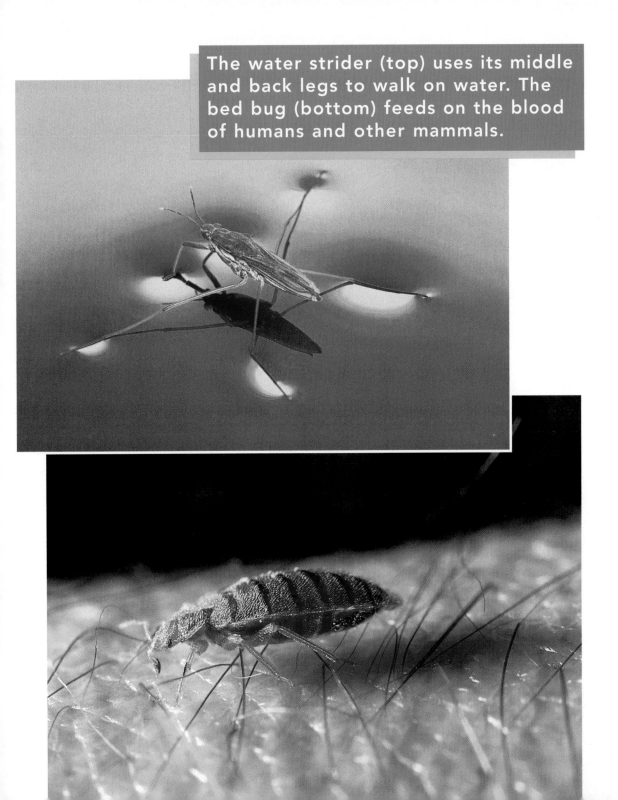

The water strider (top) uses its middle and back legs to walk on water. The bed bug (bottom) feeds on the blood of humans and other mammals.

Can you find the walking stick in this photograph?

dung, hair, and skin. Some even eat pepper.

Many insects run or fly away from enemies. Others blend in with their surroundings. When a walking stick rests on a tree, it is very hard to spot. Some insects, such as bees, have bright warning colors. A bee's yellow-and-black stripes tell enemies that it is dangerous. Once a predator gets stung, it remembers to stay

It is easy to see how the lacewing got its name.

away. Bombardier beetles shower their enemies with a stinging spray. Lacewings give off a stinky smell.

Insects and More Insects

All insects lay eggs, and they lay lots of them. A female housefly may lay up to 900 eggs at once. In just 2 weeks, the eggs have hatched and become adults that can lay more eggs. If all these flies lived, Earth would be covered with a layer of flies in just 3 months.

This female housefly is laying eggs.

Our planet isn't crawling with flies, though. That's because most fly eggs never hatch. Many of the young flies that do hatch never become adults. Some are eaten by other animals. Others starve because they cannot find enough food.

Young insects have many different names. Young beetles are called grubs. Young flies are called maggots. Young moths and butterflies are called caterpillars. All young insects are called either nymphs or larvae (LAR-vay), depending on the changes they go through to become adults.

Dragonfly nymphs (top) have no wings.
When they crawl out of their old exoskeleton
(bottom), they develop wings.

Grasshoppers, mayflies,
roaches, damsel flies, and
dragonflies have three different

36

stages during their lives. When a young grasshopper hatches from its egg, it is called a nymph. Nymphs often look similar to adults, but they have no wings. The wings slowly grow as the insect breaks out of its old exoskeleton and grows a new one.

Butterflies, moths, beetles, flies, bees, wasps, and ants have four different life stages. When a young butterfly hatches from its egg, it is called a larva. Because a butterfly larva and

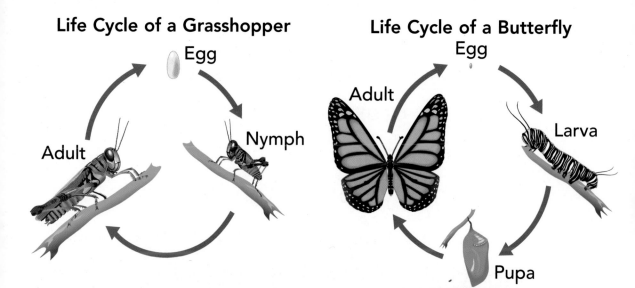

Life Cycle of a Grasshopper

Egg

Nymph

Adult

Life Cycle of a Butterfly

Egg

Larva

Pupa

Adult

There are two different patterns that insects can follow as they develop. Some insects, such as a grasshopper, have three life stages. Other insects, such as a butterfly, have four life stages.

an adult butterfly look so different, people once thought they were two different insects. They called the larva a caterpillar. When a larva is full grown, it changes into a pupa. During the pupa stage, the insect's body parts are rearranged to become an adult.

These photographs show three of the four life stages of a monarch butterfly. From left to right: larva, pupa, adult.

Insects in Our Lives

Insects play an important role in our lives. Some are harmful to people. Many insects eat crops before farmers can harvest them. Boll weevils destroy cotton crops, Colorado potato beetles eat potatoes, and earworms munch on corn. Termites eat our homes. Flies

This earworm is eating an ear of corn.

and mosquitoes can give us deadly diseases. Fleas attack our pets.

A lot of insects seem like bad guys, but many others make our lives better. If insects did not carry pollen from one plant to another, we would have no apples, strawberries, carrots, or cabbages. Without bees we would have no honey. Insects are also an important source of food for many birds, snakes, and lizards. They even help break down dead plants and animals. Without insects, our world would be a very different place.

As a honeybee feeds on nectar, it carries pollen from flower to flower.

To Find Out More

Here are some additional resources to help you learn more about insects:

 **Books**

Booth, Jerry. **Big Bugs.** Harcourt Brace, 1994.

Brimner, Larry Dane. **Bees.** Children's Press, 1999.

_____. **Butterflies and Moths.** Children's Press, 1999.

Landau, Elaine. **Minibeasts as Pets.** Children's Press, 1997.

Miller, Sara Swan. **Flies: From Flower Flies to Mosquitoes.** Franklin Watts, 1998.

_____. **True Bugs: When Is a Bug Really a Bug?** Franklin Watts, 1998.

Mound, Laurence. **Amazing Insects.** Knopf, 1993.

Wilsdon, Christina. **National Audubon Society First Field Guide to Insects.** Scholastic, Inc., 1997.

💡 Organizations and Online Sites

Bug Club

http://www.ex.ac.uk/ bugclub

This site has a list of insect experts that you can contact by e-mail. The club also organizes local field trips and publishes a newsletter six times a year.

Children's Butterfly Site

http://www.mesc.usgs.gov/ butterfly/butterfly.html

This site answers many common questions about butterflies and moths and includes information about their life cycles.

Edible Insects

http://www.eatbug.com/

Does the thought of mealworms make your mouth water? Do you think of crickets as a tasty treat? You've probably never thought about eating insects, but a look at this website may make you think again.

Young Entomologist's Society, Inc.

6901 West Grand River
  Avenue
Lansing, MI 48906

This organization has a variety of publications and outreach programs for young people interested in insects.

Yucky Bug World

http://www.yucky.com/ roaches/

If you're interested in roaches, this is the site for you. You can learn about their body structure, see photos of various roaches, and more.

Important Words

abdomen the back section of an insect's body

antenna a structure on an insect's head that helps it understand its surroundings; plural antennae

arachnid a group of animals that includes spiders, ticks, mites, scorpions, and horseshoe crabs

exoskeleton the hard material that covers and protects an insect's body

larva a young insect with a four-stage life cycle, plural larvae

nymph a young insect with a three-stage life cycle

predator an animal that kills and eats other animals for food

pupa the stage in an insect's life when it changes from a larva into an adult

thorax the middle section of an insect's body

Index

Meet the Author

Melissa Stewart earned a Bachelor's Degree in biology from Union College and a Master's Degree in Science and Environmental Journalism from New York University. She has been writing about science and nature for almost a decade. Ms. Stewart lives in Danbury, Connecticut.